F-16 FIGHTING FALCON

PETER R. FOSTER

IAN ALLAN LTD

Previous page:

PACAF saw introduction of the F–16 at an early stage, with the 8th TFW at Kunsan in South Korea receiving early Block 10 aircraft. These were soon replaced with Block 15 aircraft incorporating many of the service modifications. As a unit the 8th has become a prime test one for Fighting Falcon operations as South Korea is considered one of the most realistic peace-time scenarios available to USAF aircrew. As an aircraft the F–16 has proved itself rugged and reliable, lending weight to its overseas sales potential. The photograph depicts 81-0675/WP of the 80th TFS just prior to lift-off.
Greg Meggs

Sole distributors for the USA

Motorbooks International
Publishers & Wholesalers Inc
Osceola, Wisconsin 54020, USA

First published 1989

ISBN 0 7110 1812 X

Published by Ian Allan Ltd, Shepperton, Surrey; and printed by Butler & Tanner Ltd, Frome and London

PREFACE

There are now some 15 operators of the General Dynamics F–16, an aircraft which, in a similar fashion to its predecessor as the low cost lightweight fighter, the F–104 Starfighter, started from humble beginnings and faced a tremendous uphill struggle to find acceptance. However unlike Kelly Johnson's 'missile with a man in it', the F–16 has gone from strength to strength; and although it costs in the region of $17 million, a copy is still considered relatively cheap by current standards.

This portfolio was conceived to portray the Fighting Falcon in operational service, but it soon became apparent that with 16 Wings alone within the United States Air Force, it would be impossible to do justice to all the users within a book of this size. Therefore I have decided to attack the problem by introducing to the connoisseurs of aviation a selection of some of the best contemporary photographs of this remarkable aeroplane presently available. Virtually all of these are in active service with units of the air forces of the United States and its NATO partners. Perhaps a follow-up at some point can do justice to some of the lesser-known users. To this end I hope the reader will find as much enjoyment in reading this publication as I have had in compiling it.

Peter Foster
Brampton

FIGHTING FALCON

Left
The 'office' as seen during work time. It is clear from this photograph that excellent visibility is offered by the one-piece bubble canopy of the F–16, a fundamental necessity for survival in a combat environment. The jet belongs to the 57th FWW and was photographed from a KC–135 over Nevada early in 1987. *Ted W. Van Geffen/IAAP*

By January 1988 somewhere in the region of 2,000 General Dynamics F–16 'Fighting Falcons' had been produced off four production lines in the United States and Europe. Its users span the world with examples on all three major continents – and two operators have gone on to prove it in combat.

Probably the most widely used fly-by-wire combat system anywhere in the world, the F–16's acceptance from the embryo stage was nevertheless nearly a traumatic experience. In the late 1960s and very early 1970s, when the dollar was far from its previous healthy position, those responsible for ensuring that the best value was obtained from an admittedly large defence budget greeted the proposal for a low cost lightweight fighter (LWF) with some considerable interest. However in opposition to such a proposal sat the US Air Force, which ultimately would have to operate any new type. It somewhat naturally was concerned that any new acquisition would seriously affect the number of McDonnell-Douglas F–15 Eagles that could be purchased, thus compromising any benefits to be gained by a low-cost lightweight fighter.

In spite of all the initial misgivings shown by the military, the F–16 as we know it was given a boost in 1974 when Secretary of Defence James Schlesinger revealed that Department of Defence proposals for the LWF envisaged the possible acquisition of a derivative of greatly enhanced capability, this being known as the ACF (Air Combat Fighter),

a type radically different from the unsophisticated and inexpensive day superiority fighter of the initial proposals. This, coupled with Schlesinger's decision to provide an additional five Tactical Fighter Wings, meant that the new fighter could be procured as well as the highly sophisticated all-weather F–15 Eagle, and disposed of virtually all resistance overnight. From then on General Dynamics' project gained momentum, the company discovering more influential supporters than it ever knew existed.

The F–16 – or rather the two YF–16 prototypes – emerged at the end of the LWF evaluation programme in January 1975 as the successful candidate. (The more sophisticated YF–17 went on to greater things as the F–18 Hornet, but that is another story.) Following the evaluation trials the prototypes were joined by a batch of 15 development aircraft, four F–16B two-seaters and 11 F–16As. At this time it was becoming clear that the F–16 was to become one of the more significant combat aircraft of the 1970s and 1980s, especially with the announcement on 11 September 1974 that the winner of the LWF competition would be ordered in quantity for the USAF.

Into Service

The first production F–16 was formally accepted by the USAF on 17 August 1978 and the first delivery to an operational unit occurred on 6 January 1979. Tasked with the introduction

Front cover
The 466th TFS, 419th TFW transitioned to the F–16 in mid–1983, drawing early 1978 fiscal aircraft from the 388th TFW on the other side of the field at Hill AFB. The unit, the first in the Air Force Reserve to receive the fighter, was also the first non-regular unit to deploy overseas under the 'Coronet' deployment programme. Captured here over Colorado is a quartet of aircraft in a neat 'Vic' formation. *Ted W. Van Geffen/IAAP*

of the Fighting Falcon into service was the 388th TFW, which had gained much glory with the venerable F-105 Thunderchief in South-East Asia and had then re-activated at the unit's home base of Hill AFB, Ogden, Utah, on the F-4D Phantom. Ogden was also chosen to become the Air Logistics Centre (ALC) for the F-16, and thus the 388th had been a logical choice to bring the aircraft into service.

The 388th's 4th Tactical Fighter Squadron was the first squadron to achieve initial operational status with the F-16, on 12 November 1980, and in March of the following year the unit took 12 aircraft as 'Coronet Falcons' to Flesland in Norway for the first of many overseas deployments. The 388th was also instrumental in adding further proof to the aircraft's capability by winning the Royal Air Force-sponsored tactical bombing competition at Lossiemouth in June 1981, defeating the RAF's Jaguar and Buccaneers as well as the USAFE's F-111Es.

Running concurrently with the 388th's re-equipment was that of the 8th TFW at Kunsan, South Korea, which began converting to Block 10 aircraft in September 1981, the first two aircraft (90397/98) having been at Hill prior to delivery in May. This was followed shortly afterwards by the 50th TFW at Hahn in West Germany which received five F-16s for maintenance training from McDill on 10 September. Prior to this the Belgian Air Force was providing four aircraft per week on cross-servicing sorties. The first European squadron to equip with the F-16 was the 313th TFS, although it was originally reported that the 496th TFS would have the honour, and it began work-up at Zaragosa in Spain, returning to Hahn as an operational unit in the spring of 1982. The aircraft assigned to Hahn were from Block 15 and these had the larger horizontal tail surfaces and inlet hardpoints for AMRAAM missiles and LANTIRN sensors. The 8th at Kunsan also traded its Block 10 aircraft for Block 15, the original airframes returning re-assigned to the 363rd TFW at Shaw AFB, South Carolina, in 1982.

The 363rd had been redesignated a TFW on 1 October 1981 and had received its first F-16A, 00528, by March 1982. The Wing's first squadron, the 17th TFS, was activated on 1 July 1982, followed by the 19th TFS on 1 April 1982. The 56th TFW at McDill was also redesignated a TTW on 1 October 1981, whilst the 31st TFW had preceded both on 30 March 1981 but was still at that time completely F-4D equipped.

Also in 1982 came the highly publicised conversion to the F-16 by the USAF's Thunderbirds display team, becoming the fourth squadron to be assigned to Nellis's 474th TFW which transitioned to the F-16 after the 56th TTW at McDill. The Thunderbirds had received their full quota of nine aircraft by September.

The first Air National Guard unit to receive the Fighting Falcon was the 157th TFS at McEntire ANGB, South California, which received 24 Block 10 aircraft mainly drawn from the Hill and McDill units. The unit completed its conversion to operational readiness by mid-1983.

AFRES was also due to receive the F-16 with the 466th TFS at Hill AFB trading in the last fighter 'Thuds' during 1983. At that time the programme for 'Reserve' and 'Guard' units to receive the F-16 included the 101st FIS at Otis ANGB, the 119th FIS at Atlantic City, the 123rd FIS at Portland and the 186th FIS at Great Falls.

In Europe, hot on the heels of the 50th TFW, came the re-equipment of the 401st TFW at Torrejon, Spain, a unit that was in the centre of delicate negotiations regarding the American presence in 1987. Initially Torrejon received Block 15 aircraft, but as happened with most units began to up-grade, re-assigning the early aircraft to Stateside units.

The continued up-grade of the aircraft avionics led to the introduction of the F-16C from Fiscal Year (FY) 83 onwards. The first unit to receive the type was the 312th TFTS at Luke AFB which formed in October 1984, whilst the 363rd TFW also began the transition to the type in November 1985, with the 33rd TFS leading the way. The Wing's 'A' models were then passed onto the 31st TTW at Homestead which at that time was still utilising the 'ZF' tail code although as far as the Fighting Falcon was concerned this was shortlived because the Wing changed to a more sensible 'HS' code on 1 December 1986. One squadron's worth of later-model FISCAL-83 F-16As were transferred to the newly-formed 432nd TFW at Misawa AB in northern Japan, although this unit too began receiving General Electric F110-engined F-16Cs with its re-equipment concurrent with the 86th TFW.

In Europe both the 50th TFW at Hahn and the 86th TFW at Ramstein were scheduled to receive the F-16C/D models and both units began transition in parallel, with the 86th receiving its first four aircraft direct from Fort Worth on 20 September 1985. These were F-16Cs 84-1238/39/40 and F-

Left
The 58th Tactical Training Wing at Luke AFB reverted to a Tactical Fighter Wing which operates two squadrons of F-16A/B aircraft and two of F-16C/D. It reports to the 832nd Air Division and, as is now a common practice, reflects this on F-16A 78-0018. This aircraft is the eighteenth production F-16A and originally saw service with the 388th TFW at Hill AFB. It is seen here at Luke AFB in May 1986. *Don Jay*

16D 84-1323. Hahn received its first C model aircraft by mid-December and this time it was the 496th TFS which began conversion first. These aircraft were all Pratt & Whitney F100-engined airframes and were destined to be the last USAF examples so equipped. From October 1986 all USAF aircraft were delivered with the General Electric F110 engine. The 86th TFW was therefore tasked with the service introduction of so engined F–16s and as a result began transferring its P & W F100-engined aircraft to the 50th TFW at Hahn.

The final unit to change to F–16 operations in Europe was the 52nd TFW at Spangdahlen which received its first F–16C on 26 March 1987. The Wing, unlike all other F–16 operators, intended to use the Fighting Falcon alongside the F–4G 'Wild Weasel' Phantoms in joint squadrons – a formation jocularly known as the 'Odd Couple'.

At home the USAF's longed-for goal of achieving 40 tactical Wings by the mid-1990s had faded to 37 because of continued budget restraints. The DoD therefore now concentrates on up-grading existing units, with Fiscal Year requests in 1988 and 1989 totalling 360 aircraft.

This up-grading continued with the 159th FIS Florida ANG receiving its first four aircraft in August 1986 along with the 182nd TFS Texas ANG at Kelly AFB, both of which were recipients of former 50th TFW F–16As. The 134th TFS Vermont ANG at Burlington also began transition from the F–4D to F–16 in mid-1986, its aircraft being predominantly former 388th TFW machines, from the de-actuated 16th TFS.

For the future, the 8th TFW at Kunsan began transition onto the F–16C in October 1987, with its 'A' models returning to the States for use by the 347th TFW at Moody AFB, whilst the 184th TFG at McConnell started to re-equip with the F–16A during the same period, the 161st TFTS activating for the purpose on 12 September 1987.

Other units scheduled to receive the F–16 included 160th TRS Alabama ANG and 184th TFS Arkansas ANG in spring 1988, and 465th TFS (the second AFRES unit) at Tinker AFB, Oklahoma. The first air defence dedicated F–16As will go to the 114th TFTS Oregon ANG at Kingsley Field in early 1989 to be followed by the 194th FIS California ANG at Fresno in late 1989.

For the first time since converting the F–86 and F–80 for carrier use, the US Navy adopted a land-based fighter when it accepted the first of 26 F–16N Fighting Falcons to replace the ageing A–4 and F–5 aircraft of the Fighter Weapons 'Top Gun' school. The first aircraft was delivered on 30 April 1987 with all 22 single-seat and four two-seat aircraft due by the end of April 1988. The F–16N is basically a C model without the M61A1 20mm cannon, and is fitted with the F–16A APG66 radar.

'Sale of the Century'

There can be little doubt that having the USAF fully committed to the ACF concept and in particular the F–16 was an initial step by both Congress and GD to the more lucrative markets of Europe and the free world. The late 1970s was seen as the time of a ripe market with many of NATO's front-line second-generation jets nearing the end of their effectiveness. GD, along with Dassault-Breguet, Saab and Northrop, was eagerly canvassing the respective defence ministries of Holland, Denmark, Norway and Belgium in the hope of securing an initial order for approximately 350 aeroplanes.

To ease the selection process the four nations formed a body known as the Multi-national Fighter Programme Group (MFPG) early in 1974. Following the evaluation of the final four contenders – F–16, F–18, Mirage F–1 and Saab Euro-fighter (a Viggen derivative) – the F–16 emerged as the front-runner. The announcement of its victory was made at the 1975 Paris Air Show.

The initial order called for 348 aircraft, made up of 290 F–16As plus 58 two-seat F–16Bs. Holland, Belgium and Denmark have increased their quantities to allow for the replacement not only of the F–104 Starfighter as originally intended but also the Northrop/Canadair F–5 and Dassault Mirage V fleets.

Delivery of the first European production aircraft was off the SABCA line at Gosselies in the shape of F–16B FB01 on 23 March 1979, and it and the subsequent aircraft to roll off the Belgian line formed into a conversion unit at Beauvechain under the auspices of No 1 Wing. On 16 January 1981 the first squadron, No 349, Belgian AF, was officially assigned to NATO, being declared operational on 6 May. This was followed by No 350 Squadron (also at Beauvechain) in the interceptor role and subsequently Nos 23 and 31 Squadrons of No 10 Wing at Kleine Brogel. Belgium's original intention was for three wings of F–16s, the final wing to be No 2 at Florennes which will consist of Nos 1 and 2 Squadrons. The

Right
With one of the great Salt Lakes in the background, F–16A 78-0027/HI of the 466th TFS begins its approach over Ogden to Hill AFB. The unit has been joined by a second AFRES unit, the 302nd TFS at Luke AFB, which, consistent with US policy of upgrading its non-regular forces, began receiving factory-fresh 86 fiscal F–16Cs in the middle of 1987. The 302nd converted from the CH-3E which it had employed in the special operations role, and it now falls under the control of the 944th TFG, both units having activated on 1 July 1987. *Ted W. Van Geffen/ IAAP*

crews are currently undergoing conversion at Beauvechain.

The second nation to receive the F–16 in Europe was Holland when F–16B J259 was rolled out at Fokker's Schipole production line on 3 May 1979, followed shortly by the first F–16A, J212, both being delivered on 6 June of that year. However, rather than operate twinned squadrons the *Koninklijke Luchtmacht* chose to shut down each of the units converting to the F–16 for the year or so that the transition required. Initially the *Transitie en Conversie Afdeling* (TCA) at Leeuwarden was set up to handle F–16 conversion with the instructors at the beginning having undergone training at Hill AFB with the 388th TFW. No 322 Squadron, chosen to be the first to convert to the type, began transition at Leeuwarden in October 1979 with the unit completing conversion by the end of April 1981. No 322 was followed by No 323, also at Leeuwarden, before a second OCU was set up at Volkel to handle the transition by Nos 306, 311 and 312 Squadrons.

The TCA at Leeuwarden stayed in situ until 1 March 1986, handling the conversion for the air defence committed units, whilst the OCU at Volkel was hidden within the structure of No 311 Squadron. This has now passed on to No 315 Squadron at Twenthe which as the sixth squadron to convert will now handle the transition of the three remaining squadrons, Nos 313, 314 and 316, as well as new pilots for the existing squadrons.

Denmark, the third country in the NATO consortium, received its first F–16 off the SABCA production line on 28 January 1980 with an initial order for 46 single-seat F–16As and 12 two-seat F–16Bs. The first units to re-equip were *Esk 727* and *Esk 730* at Skrydstrup, phasing out the ageing F–100 Super Sabres. *Esk 727*, the first to transition, was declared operational to NATO on 26 August 1981.

During the work-up, Denmark, akin to the other NATO users, had four instructors trained at Hill AFB. They then formed the nucleus of the first unit. However, unlike Holland, Denmark split the unit into two, operating the two types alongside one another and thus maintaining *Esk 727*'s operational capability.

Once the Skrydstrup Wing had completed its transition it was then the turn of Aalborg and the F–104 Starfighter. *Esk 723* was the first to receive the Fighting Falcon but it was the CF–104Gs that were phased out – the MAP F–104Gs being passed to *Esk 726*. This unit in turn completed its conversion to the F–16 with the last Starfighter sortie taking place on 30 April 1986.

Norway, as the final user, drew its F–16s from the Fokker production line and had a requirement for 60 F–16A and 12 F–16B aircraft. This small force was intended to fulfil a requirement for a weapons system capable of area defence and anti-invasion strikes, but the numbers ordered were not sufficient to protect all airfields.

The *Kongelige Norske Luftforsvaret* (RNorAF) received its first aircraft on 25 January 1980 and the intention was to re-equip four squadrons. A former F–5 user, *332 Skv*, was chosen to become the OCU and was fully equipped with the F–16 by the autumn of 1981. The first operational unit was *331 Skv* at Bodo, an air defence squadron which drew its aircraft from the enlarged *332 Skv* at Rygge. The second operational unit was *334 Skv* which was Norway's anti-shipping CF–104 unit armed with the Bullpup missile, although it too had been equipped with the F–5 until the middle 1970s. Then *334 Skv* began receiving its F–16s from the second production batch, the aircraft being delivered on 26 June 1982. Following its work-up *331 Skv* traded in its early model aircraft for the latest batch, returning the former to Rygge.

The final unit scheduled to receive the F–16 was originally mooted as *338 Skv* at Orland, but it was *336 Skv* at Rygge that started to transition to the type in 1984. However in 1985 the decision was reversed and *338 Skv* became the fourth squadron although the prevailing shortage of pilots and aircraft in Norway has resulted in the unit establishment being far from acceptable.

The Export Game

In the early stages of the F–16 programme the USAF opposed early delivery commitments being made to nations outside the European consortium, with the exception of Iran. This was to avoid a shortage of aircraft and spares, the service not wanting to see any other export commitments until 1981. Nevertheless, with the downfall of the Shah, Israel was quick to gain from those aircraft already on line for Iran. This block of aircraft ran from 78–0308 to 78–0467 with the IDF taking up the initial 56 airframes, the residue being cancelled. The first five aircraft, all F–16Bs, were delivered to Ramat-David Air Base on a direct flight from Pease AFB on 2 July 1980. Israel

Left
Serving alongside the AFRES unit at Luke AFB are the F–15s of the 405th TTW and the F–16s of the 58th TFW as illustrated by this aircraft, 78-0058/LF. The 'LF' tail code stands for Luke Falcon whereas that carried by the 302nd TFS/AFRES is 'LR' for Luke Reserve. *Peter R. Foster collection*

saw the great potential of the F–16 and has gone on to order a further 20 F–16As and 148 F–16C/Ds. It is one of the few countries to use the jet in anger.

In spite of the USAF's resistance to early overseas sales, the GD team was quick to snap up sales opportunities. Egypt became the first customer after Iran and was quickly followed by Pakistan, both ordering the F–16A/B models. GD, in an attempt to attract less well-off countries, converted one of the pre-production aircraft – 50747 – to the F–16/J79 version, later redesignated F–16E, and this first flew at Fort Worth on 29 October 1980. This has, however, had virtually no effect, with interested countries being prepared to accept fewer airframes at normal production standard rather than more of a slightly inferior model.

Venezuela was the next customer to receive the F–16A. The 24 aircraft spread over two years have been used to equip *161* and *162 Esquadron Group de Caza 16* at Base Aerienne Liberator at Palo Negro. South Korea ordered 36 of the F–16C/D derivative in an attempt to up-grade its air force, the first aircraft being assigned to the 161st TFS at Teagu in 1986. This was followed by the forming of the 162nd TFS, also at Teagu, on 1 November 1987.

In Europe, Turkey concluded an agreement for the supply of 160 F–16C/Ds with GD supplying the initial 10 airframes and the rest being produced locally by TUSAS at Murted. The first GD aircraft arrived at Murted aboard a C-5A Galaxy in May 1987.

In an attempt to maintain the uneasy peace between NATO's two southern partners, Congress authorised the sale of 40 F–16Gs direct from GD to Greece with deliveries to begin at the end of 1988. This agreement was finally signed on 12 January 1986, the delay a result of arguments on offset terms.

In the Far East, Singapore was initially the only country to show interest in the F–16/J79, ordering four single-seat and four two-seat aircraft in 1984. However, following US approval

for the sale of production standard aircraft to Thailand in 1985, Singapore sought and gained approval itself for an upgrade with initial delivery for 1988.

Indonesia is the final confirmed Far Eastern customer for 12 F–16A/Bs, these powered by the P & W F100/220 engine for delivery in mid-1989.

Jordan has shown considerable interest in the F–16, but if rumours of a MiG–29 sale are correct then there is little likelihood of the Fighting Falcon finding its way into Jordanian colours. Nearer home, Switzerland is looking for the Mirage III's replacement and the F–16C was one of the aircraft under consideration.

With development costs running so high for new high-technology aircraft, and the cancellation of the Lavi project, Israel is likely to purchase further F–16s, whilst the Japanese Self Defence Force has settled upon the F–16 to fulfil its FSX requirements. A total of 130 aircraft are required for the JASDF at a unit cost of $30 million, with modifications to include a larger composite construction wing with radar absorbent leading edge, stretched fuselage, ventral fins under the intake, strengthened cockpit canopy, active phased array radar and updated mission avionics and computer.

GD in its wisdom has proposed an upgraded version of the F–16 called Agile Falcon. The proposal to the USAF would involve a five-nation production programme combining two already proposed USAF propulsion and avionics upgrades complete with a larger wing and composite material components. Improvements would include better manoeuvrability and landing performance, plus greater payload and range.

A decision by 1990 would enable deliveries to commence to the participating nations – with the project directed at NATO – by 1995. Whatever the future holds, we are certain to see the F–16 as one of the most widely-used fighter types since the advent of the F–86. It will be around well into the next century.

Right
Photographed from a Utah ANG KC–135E in 1982, F–16B 78-0086/HL of the 421st TFS can be seen over the Rockies prior to a range sortie. On the port outer station are practice bombs whilst the 421st Squadron name 'Black Widows' is clearly seen in the fin band. This particular aircraft was transferred to the 58th TFW at Luke AFB shortly after this photograph was taken. *Ted W. Van Geffen/IAAP*

Far right
Another F–16B to be delivered factory fresh to the 388th TFW in 1979 was 78-0088/HL. Seen from Hill AFB's high control tower, this particular aircraft was transferred to the 58th TFW as the 388th TFW began receiving Block 15 aircraft. It has since been passed on to the 6512th Test Squadron/AFFTC at Edwards AFB where it carries the 'ED' tail code. *Peter R. Foster*

Above right
Subsequently not adopted, this experimental lizard colour scheme was displayed on 388th TFW F–16B 80096/HL during 1982. At that time the jet was operated by the 34th TFS, as conveyed by its red fin band; it is pictured here at Eglin AFB. In the background can be seen a C–141A in another scheme, almost forgotten. *Ted W. Van Geffen/IAAP*

Below right
In a more normal scheme for No 350 Squadron, BAF FB03 carries the red fin band and Gaul's head, whilst it will be noted that this particular aircraft has not been retrofitted with the redesigned tail cone. In October 1987 the conversion flight at Beauvechain was upgraded to squadron level which led to redistribution of the Wing's F–16s. As a result, both Nos 349 and 350 Squadrons received 'B' model aircraft whereas these particular machines had previously been common user and were devoid of unit insignia. *Peter R. Foster*

Left
The TCA (*Transitie en Conversie Afdeling*) at Leeuwarden was formed initially to introduce pilots into the F-16 world but later undertook conversion to the air defence role. This part of the F–16 syllabus is now incorporated in the general *Klu* F–16 conversion and therefore the TCA was de-activated on 1 March 1986. Here, with its distinctive blue badge, is F–16B J271 which has the distinction of being the only two-seater to be lost by the Royal Netherlands Air Force. *Herman J. Sixma/IAAP*

Far left
The first occasion that the Danish Air Force participated in a major UK exercise with a significant number of F–16s was 'Mallet Blow 1/83'. On that occasion *Esk 727/730* detached 10 aircraft to RAF Coltishall for the duration of what had previously been an in-house exercise. Not a country to have, in recent times, displayed more than the bare minimum in unit markings, individual identification of Danish aircraft is sometimes only possible by close scrutiny of the patch on the pilot's arm. The jets do however usually carry the squadron badge on the intake beneath the cockpit, although this particular example does not. *Peter R. Foster*

Left
The Fighting Falcon is perhaps one of the best close combat fighters in existence today. However, even the most confident F–16 pilot can be given a rude awakening by the versatile British Aerospace Hawk's superb manoeuvrability. Therefore *Klu* aircraft are regularly detached to Decimomannu to pit themselves against the RAF's ADV units, whilst both Nos 322 and 323 Squadrons set up regular detachments to RAF Brawdy for DACT with No 79 Squadron. Here J254 of No 323 Squadron can be seen being escorted back to Brawdy by XX222 and XX317. *Robbie Shaw*

Right

**Holland was the second user
of the F-16 in Europe. Now that
the TCA at Leeuwarden has
de-activated the surviving
F–16Bs of Holland's initial
order, J259–J271 have been re-
distributed between the
Wing's two squadrons
bringing them back up to
strength after the loss of some
10 aircraft in the 10 years of
operation. Here J262/78-0262
is seen at the hammerhead
prior to departure from
Leeuwarden in April 1984.**
Herman J. Sixma/IAAP

Far right

**The Royal Norwegian Air
Force became a member of
the F–16 club with the delivery
of 272/78-0272 in mid-1979.
The first operational unit was
332 Skv based at Rygge, which
also serves as the operational
conversion unit. Here 274
displays 332's fin flash at RAF
Alconbury in August 1987. It
will also be noticed that this
aircraft has the lengthened tail
housing which is built as
standard on all Norwegian
machines and contains a
brake landing chute
considered essential on the
icy runways in the far north.**
Peter R. Foster

Right

Impressive at any time, the snow-covered Rocky Mountains create a fabulous backdrop to these two F–16As from the 421st TFS whilst on a sortie from Hill AFB. Both the jets pictured here have gone on to see service with the reserves, 78-0039 moving down the ramp to join the 466th TFS/AFRES and 79-0294 joining the 152nd TFS, the first Air National Guard unit to operate the type. *Ted W. Van Geffen/IAAP*

Far right

South Carolina became the first guard unit to adopt the F–16A, during mid–1983. The 157th TFS traded its reliable A–7D Corsair IIs in for 24 F–16As drawn primarily from the 388th TFW and retained its familiar 'SC' code. The unit, which has regularly in the past deployed to RAF Wittering, has yet to cross the Atlantic with its Falcons but this is no doubt just a matter of time. *Peter R. Foster collection*

Far left
The 474th TFW at Nellis AFB became the first front-line F–16 Wing within the USA. It was eventually joined by the 388th TFW when it lost its training commitment, but it has fallen to the Nellis units to supply much of the European re-deployment with one of its prime forward operating locations being RAF Bentwaters in Suffolk. Here a pair of F–16As from 428th TFS 'Buccaneers' await their slot time prior to the 'Coronet Re-deploy' on 6 July 1984. *Peter R. Foster*

Above left
The first unit within the structure of the USAF to receive the F–16 Fighting Falcon was of course the Air Force Flight Test Center (AFFTC) and in particular the 6512th TS. Aircraft operating from 'Ted's place' (as Edwards AFB is often referred to) have in the past been pretty anonymous although in the last couple of years have begun receiving the 'ED' tail code. *Peter R. Foster collection*

Below left
The prime test establishment units to utilise the F–16 are those associated with the ADTC at Eglin AFB. The two prime units at this location are the 3246th TW (coded 'AD'), and the 4485th TS (coded 'OT') with whom this example operates. F–16 80-0551 is seen at Tyndall AFB in October 1982. *Peter R. Foster collection*

Far left
**Former 10th TFS, 50th TFW
mount 80-0591 was delivered
to the 134th TFS Vermont ANG
in mid-1986, which drew its
aircraft from the 388th TFW
with which this particular
airframe briefly served
following its relocation from
Hahn AB. The unit reverted to
a fighter unit from its previous
role of electronic
countermeasures training with
the EB–57B, utilising the F–4D
Phantom for a brief period.
Transition to the F–16 has
created yet another slot where
Weapon System Operators
have found themselves
without a job – a problem that
will only be relieved with the
introduction of the F–15E
Strike Eagle.** *Peter R. Foster
collection*

Left
**Seen against a very black sky
F–16A 80-0613 from the 10th
TFS, 50th TFW completes its
landing at RAF Alconbury on
21 September 1984. Many of
the 'A' model Falcons
assigned to the Wing at Hahn
were, when relocated to the
States, passed on to the Guard
units at Tucson, San Antonio
and Jacksonville.** *Peter R.
Foster*

Right
Apart from the 'Red Flag' exercises, Nellis AFB also hosts 'Gun Smoke' in which units eagerly compete for the various honours. Each command holds its own fly-off and USAFE has regularly been represented by the 50th TFW at Hahn, which provides a joint team. Here several 'A' models can be seen amongst the ordnance during the 1986 meet, the last the Wing was to undertake prior to upgrading with the heavier and more sophisticated 'C' model.
Cor de Blij via Ben Ullings

Below right
NATO countries have been regular participants in 'Red Flag' exercises following the example set by the RAF in the late 1970s. Here No 23 'Smaldeel' Belgian Air Force F–16As can be seen with RF-4Cs from the 26th TRW at Zweibrucken during one of the 1986 'Flag' exercises. *Cor de Blij via Ben Ullings*

Far right
Proving that variety is the spice of life, No 23 'Smaldeel', 10 Wing F–16A FA67 lines up with an F–4C from *Esquadron 122* of the Spanish Air Force at Kleine Brogel on 31 March 1987. NATO exchanges provide an opportunity for crews to discuss and practice tactics which prove to be mutually helpful. Spain is of course upgrading its own forces with the hi-tech EF–18.
Pieter Van Gamert via Ben Ullings

Right

No 23 'Smaldeel's' sister unit at Kleine Brogel is of course the renowned 31 'Tigers'. In this shot, taken from a struggling CM 170 Magister, all four of the 31 jets are crewed by 23 'Smaldeel' pilots. This practice is common throughout the Belgian Air Force, with aircrew being split into two flights but squadron ground personnel being drawn from the Wing; therefore one line will operate the day shift and the other the evening. The net result is an exchange of mounts. *Peter R. Foster*

Far right

Denmark phased out its ageing F–100 Super Sabres before beginning transition of its air defence F–104 Starfighters. *Esk 723* at Skrydstrup was the first to trade in the venerable old lady to be followed some two years later by *Esk 726*. E596 (80-3596) is seen here at Aalborg in June 1985 set amongst the overgrown conditions which abound on most of the Danish bases. *Peter R. Foster*

Right
E596 displays its clean lines at the Alconbury air day in 1987. With 29 squadrons operating the type within Europe it is not surprising that the display scene becomes somewhat over-populated with the type. It is interesting to watch the performance of the different pilots in an aircraft which helps even the average look like aces. *Peter R. Foster*

Far right
This fine study of J616 of 311 Squadron of the *Klu* illustrated a special scheme devised for the *Klu* 1986 open day. The Dutch Air Force has a requirement for a total of 213 F–16s to replace F–104G Starfighters and NF–5 Freedom Fighters. To date six units have fully re-equipped, leaving 313 Squadron on Twenthe under transition with 314 and 316 to follow. *Ben Ullings/API*

Far left
No 315 Squadron *Klu*'s first F–16 was this 'B' model. J653 was on loan to the unit in 1984 from No 306 Squadron prior to the delivery of the FY83 aircraft which have gone to make the unit's equipment. *Herman J. Sixma/IAAP*

Left
South-East Asia still places great demands on the PACAF in participation of exercises like 'Cope Thunder', 'Cope Jade', 'Team Spirit' and 'Pitch Black'. These exercises are helping to bring together some of the smaller non-Communist countries as a viable force capable of working together to maintain stability in the region. Here the 8th TFW Commander's aircraft, 81-0728/WP, can be seen during a 'Pitch Black' exercise with RNZAF A–4 Skyhawks in the background. *Greg Meggs*

Right
As the Red Arrows with the BAe Hawk, the USAF Thunderbirds team has been a fine emissary not only for the country but also for the F–16 sales drive. The unit (which in a war role is assigned to the 474th TFW and does periodically maintain its capability) equipped with the Fighting Falcon in 1982 following the loss of four T–38 Talons in a training accident. Since equipping with the type its safety record has been excellent, something it has never attained with any other type save perhaps the F–100 Super Sabre. *USAF*

Far right
The F–16B is used extensively in the training role, but is considered by most pilots to be one of the most uncomfortable aircraft to ride back-seat due to its incredible manoeuvrability leaving even the most hardened stomach thinking of other things. Although most front-line squadrons maintain a couple of examples on strength, they serve no real purpose other than for incentive and orientation rides. These aircraft are used on normal sorties just as much as the single-seat versions – sometimes with and sometimes without the back seat being occupied. Here 81-0818 of the 10th TFS, 50th TFW lands at RAF Alconbury, with a menacing cloud formation in the background. *Peter R. Foster*

Far left
Holland's fifth squadron to re-equip with the F–16A, and final F–104 Starfighter operator, was 312 Squadron at Volkel which began the transition in 1983. The unit is equipped with the bulk of the FY81 aircraft and is easily identified by its distinctive badge consisting of a black disc with two crossed golden swords and a red lightning flash. The example depicted is 81-0871, seen at RAF Coningsby during a UK air defence exercise in October 1985. *Peter R. Foster*

Left
One of the most interesting USAF operators of the type is the 57th FWW at Nellis AFB on the outskirts of Las Vegas. The unit is responsible for the development of tactics and the operational introduction of new weapons, and serves in a similar role to the RAF's Operational Evaluation Units (OEU). The unit at Nellis operates both the A and B versions whilst Detachment II at Luke AFB is responsible for service evaluation of the F–16C and D models. Here F–16A 82-0910/WA drops away following a refuelling from a KC–135E of the Utah ANG. *Ted W. Van Geffen/IAAP*

Right
KC–135s are essential to the redeployment of US forces to Europe and the Far East, whilst they also enhance training within the US itself. They provide the photographer with an ideal photo platform, with the boom operator's position an excellent vantage point. Here 57th FWW F–16B 82-1033/WA is seen off the tanker's starboard quarter. It is carrying a centre-line fuel tank, a luggage pod on the port station and an AIM–9 acquisition round on the wing-tip rail. *Ted W. Van Geffen/IAAP*

Far right
Although it has been common practice over many years for squadron commanders to 'specialise' their aircraft, in recent times Wing commanders and Air Division commanders have followed suit and, as can be seen on this 363 TFW F–16B, 82-1041/SW, also the 9th Air Force commander. As often happens when such high-ranking officers deign to fly, it is always the specially-marked aircraft that is assigned to them. One result is that several aircraft receive such markings to ensure that one is always available. *Regent Dansereau*

Right
On the theme of special schemes, F–16A 83-1076/HS is specially marked as the 31st TFW commander's mount. The luggage pod on the outer port station carries the inscription of Col H. Hale Burr, the unit's commander. This particular Wing still operates the F–4D alongside the F–16, whilst it had the only squadron to deactivate on the type, the 306th TFS. *Don Jay*

Far right
The latest USAF Wing to equip with the F–16 is the 347th TFW at Moody AFB, Georgia. This particular aircraft, 83-1107, carries no fin code and is the commander's aeroplane. It was also drawn from the source of the last F–16As produced for the USAF and was previously assigned to the 13th TFS, 432nd TFW at Misawa in Japan. The Wing is currently still re-equipping, with many of its aircraft coming from the 8th TFW which is presently transitioning to the F–16C.
Don Jay

Far left
The 13th TFS, 432nd TFW at Misawa, Japan, only operated the F–16A for a short period during which time it lost only one aircraft. That machine, 83-1115, is depicted here specially marked as the Wing commander's mount. Its remains currently reside on the dump at Misawa AB. *USAF*

Left
On exercise, this Dutch F–16A, J193 (83-1193) from 311 Squadron, is seen landing at RAF Lakenheath to where it had been detached for the period of the UK air defence exercise 'Priory 2/87'. It will be noticed that the aircraft also sports a red/white checkered fin stripe acquired during its detachment to CFB Goose Bay for low level training. *Peter R. Foster*

Far left
When the 86th TFW at Ramstein began its transition to the F–16C, two F–16s were adorned with special marks, the first being the 86th TFW commander's aircraft (84-1286) which received this striking red/white striped tail reminiscent of the days of the Sabre. However, unlike those days when such markings were commonplace, anyone flying this jet became a target to all the other hungry fighter jocks in Germany. *Herman J. Sixma/IAAP*

Left
The other F–16 to be specially marked at Ramstein was 84-1316 which received these marks for the commander of the 316th Air Division. Neither jet now serves with the Wing as both squadrons up-graded to GE F110-engined aircraft before operational capability was achieved. *Herman J. Sixma/IAAP*

Right

Although the engining of F–16s with the F110 began with the FY85 block of aircraft initially, aircraft within that order came off the Fort Worth production line in an either/or state with those aircraft fitted with the P & W F100 engine being assigned to the 50th TFW at Hahn AB. Here a versatile example, 85-1418/HR, is put through its paces at Alconbury during August 1987. *Peter R. Foster*

Far right

Although the 86th TFW initially received P & W F100-engined F-16Cs, the unit soon had GE F110-engined machines delivered as US policy to get away before an all Pratt & Whitney-engined force took effect. Its former F100-engined machines were gradually transferred to the 50th TFW at Hahn AB and 363th TFW at Shaw AFB in the USA. The first squadron for the 86th was originally thought to be the 417th TFS but in fact these jets were for the 512 th TFS which received a different fin tip band. The second unit was the 526th TFS, which began receiving its FY85 aircraft in late 1986/early 1987. *Peter R. Foster*

Far left
Departing RAF Alconbury at the end of its display routine, F–16C 85-1418/HR and its sister aircraft, 85-1399/HR, make an attractive paired take-off from runway 30. It will be noted that both aircraft are assigned to the 10th TFS but that the blue fin band and 'HR' tail code of '418' have gold highlights specially adopted for the USAF's 'Gun Smoke' gunnery meet held at Nellis AFB. *Peter R. Foster*

Left
Having traded in F100-engined 84-1286, the 86th TFW commander adopted 85-1426 with a revised marking. The jet is held on the strength of the 526th TFS whilst that painted for the 316th Air Division commander appears on 512th's strength. '426' appeared outside its shelter in June 1987 displaying a full load of AIM-9M Sidewinder missiles. *Peter R. Foster*

Right
Following the 432nd TFW in receiving the F110-engined F–16C is the 8th TFW at Kunsan in South Korea. By November 1987 the Wing had received eight examples and the first squadron, the 35th TFS, was expected to complete transition during January 1988. Here 86-0207/WP taxies beneath the control tower at Kunsan. *Peter R. Foster*

Far right
Whilst the 86th TFW was in transition from the F–4E Phantom to the F–16C its alert commitment was maintained by Air National Guard F–4D Phantoms under a detachment called 'Creek Party'. The Phantoms were drawn from North Dakota, California and Minnesota, remaining on alert for over 12 months whilst the crews were rotated at regular intervals. The extra length of deployment was caused by the 86th's service introduction of the F110 in the F–16. Here refuelling from a KC-135 over Germany are a pair of F–4D Phantoms and F–16D 85-1511/RS from the 526th TFS. *Ted W. Van Geffen/IAAP*

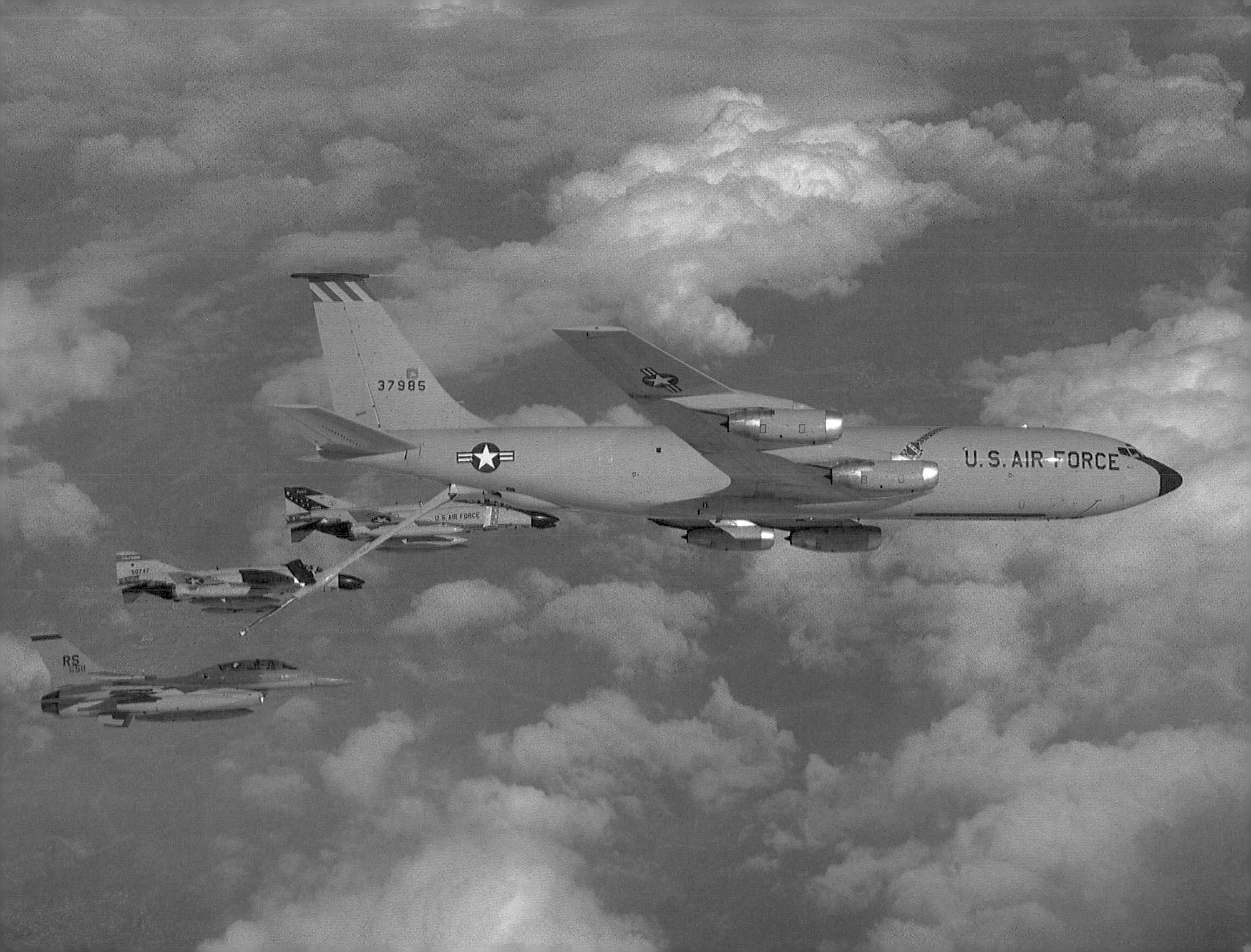
37985
U.S. AIR FORCE
U.S. AIR FORCE
RS

Right
The Dutch were the first of the European consortium to employ KC–135s for IFR practice and now detach to CFB Goose Bay on a regular basis for low-level training. The ground attack units have also deployed to Nellis AFB for a 'Red Flag' detachment and No 306 Squadron should have, by the time this book is published, taken part in the 1988 Reconnaissance Air Meet at Bergstrom AFB. Here nicely captured over a clear North Sea in May 1985 is F–16B J270 of No 323 Squadron.
Robbie Shaw

Far right
Engine running ... ground crew complete final checks before permission to taxi is given. Here F–16C 85-1570/MJ of the 14th TFS, 432nd TFW, is prepared for a mission at Misawa AB in November 1987.
Peter R. Foster

Far left
Main checks complete ... ground crew await the Inertial Navigation System to settle down before waving the jet off the pan. The same procedures are adopted whether regular or reserve units; here 466th TFS F–16As prepare for a sortie. *Ted W. Van Geffen/IAAP*

Left
Pan checks complete and INS aligned, aircraft taxi to the 'last chance' where the armourer awaits to remove the arming pins from the weapons load. *Ted W. Van Geffen*

Right
A RNorAF pilot runs through his pre start-up checks prior to a sortie. This view illustrates well the smooth contours of the one-piece canopy. *Allan Burney*

Far right
The 401st commander's F–16A was one of the first to be seen in Europe sporting rather more attractive marks. Here the jet, 82-0977/TJ, is displayed at the Alconbury air day in 1986 wearing a high visibilty unit badge, the squadron colours around the intake and the name *El Conquistador*. *Peter R. Foster*

APPENDIX

F–16 SERIALS

Model	Serials	Notes
YF–16	72–01567–8	
F–16A	75–0745–750	50745 was F–16–101DFE, 50747 to F–16E, 50749 to F–16XL, 50750 to F–16AFTI (Listed as NF–16A in official inventory)
F–16B	75–0751–752	
F–16A	78–0001–027	
F–16A	78–0038–076	
F–16B	78–0077–115	
F–16A	78–0116–161	FMS Belgium FA01–FA46
F–16B	78–0162–173	FMS Belgium FB01–FB12
F–16A	78–0174–203	FMS Denmark E174–E203
F–16B	78–0204–211	FMS Denmark ET204–ET211
F–16A	78–0212–258	FMS Netherlands J212–J258
F–16B	78–0259–271	FMS Netherlands J259–J271
F–16A	78–0272–300	FMS Norway 272–300
F–16B	78–0301–307	FMS Norway 301–307
F–16A	78–0308–354	FMS Israel 100/102/105/107/ 109/111–114/116/118/121/124/ 126/129/131/135/138/219/220/222/ 223/225/227/228/230/232–234/ 236/237/239/240/242/243/246/ 248/249/250/252/254/255/257/ 258/260/261/264–267/269/272– 277/281/282/284/285/287/290/ 292/296/298/299
F–16B	78–0355–362	FMS Israel 001/003/004/006/008/010/ 015/017
F–16	78–0363–467	FMS Iran – cancelled
F–16A	79–0288–409	
F–16B	79–0410–432	
F–16A	80–0474–622	
F–16B	80–0623–638	
F–16A	80–0639–643	FMS Egypt 9301–9305
F–16B	80–0644–648	FMS Egypt 9201–9205
F–16A	80–0649–668	FMS Israel
F–16A	80–3538–587	FMS Belgium FA47–FA96
F–16B	80–3588–595	FMS Belgium FB13–FB20
F–16A	80–3596–611	FMS Denmark E596–E611
F–16B	80–3612–615	FMS Denmark ET612–ET615
F–16A	80–3616–648	FMS Netherlands J616–J648
F–16B	80–3649–657	FMS Netherlands J649–J657
F–16A	80–3658–688	FMS Norway 658–688
F–16B	80–3689–693	FMS Norway 689–693
F–16C	80–3694–744	FMS Israel
F–16D	80–3745–768	FMS Israel
F–16A	81–0643–661	FMS Egypt 9306–9323
F–16B	81–0662	FMS Egypt 9206
F–16A	81–0663–811	
F–16B	81–0812–822	
F–16A	81–0864–881	FMS Netherlands J864–J881
F–16B	81–0882	FMS Netherlands J882
F–16B	81–0883	FMS Egypt 9207
F–16B	81–0884–885	FMS Netherlands J884–J885
F–16	81–0899–938	FMS Pakistan (including 28 F–16As and 12 F–16Bs)

F–16A	82–0900–1026	
F–16B	82–1027–049	
F–16A	82–1050–052	FMS Venezuela 1041, 0051, 6611
F–16B	82–1053–055	FMS Venezuela 1715, 2179, 9581
F–16A	82–1056–065	FMS Egypt 9324–9334
F–16A	83–1066–117	
F–16C	83–1118–165	
F–16B	83–1166–173	
F–16D	83–1174–185	
F–16A	83–1186–188	FMS Venezuela 8900, 0678, 3260
F–16B	83–1189–191	FMS Venezuela 2337, 7635, 9583
F–16A	83–1192–207	FMS Netherlands J192–J207
F–16B	83–1208–211	FMS Netherlands J208–J211
F–16C	84–1212–318	
F–16D	84–1319–331	
F–16C	84–1332–341	FMS Egypt
F–16D	84–1342–345	FMS Egypt
F–16A	84–1346–357	FMS Venezuela 7268, 9068, 8924, 0094, 6023, 4226, 5422, 6426, 4827, 9864, 3648, 0220
F–16A	84–1358–367	FMS Netherlands J358–J367
F–16B	84–1368–369	FMS Netherlands J368–J369
F–16D	84–1370–373	FMS South Korea
F–16C	84–1374–395	
F–16D	84–1396–397	
F–16A	85–0135–141	FMS Netherlands J135–J141
F–16B	85–0142	FMS Netherlands J142
F–16A	85–0143–145	FMS Netherlands J143–J145
F–16C	85–1398–505	
F–16D	85–1506–517	
F–16C	85–1544–570	
F–16D	85–1571–573	
F–16C	85–1574–583	FMS South Korea
F–16D	85–1584–585	FMS South Korea
F–16D	86–0039–052	
F–16	86–0054–065	FMS Netherlands
F–16C	86–0066–???	FMS Turkey to at least 069
F–16A	86–0073–077	FMS Belgium FA97–FA101
F–16D	86–0191–???	FMS Turkey to at least 194
F–16B	86–0197–199	FMS Denmark ET197–ET199
F–16C	86–0207–371	
F–16C	86–1586–597	FMS South Korea
F–16B	87–0001	FMS Belgium FB21
F–16A	87–0004–008	FMS Denmark E004–E008
F–16B	87–0022	FMS Denmark ET022
F–16A	87–0046–056	FMS Belgium FA102–FA112
F–16	87–0057–068	FMS Netherlands canx
F–16B	87–0401–0404	FMS Singapore

F–16A	87–0508–514	FMS Netherlands
F–16B	87–0515–516	FMS Netherlands
F–16C	87–1653–660	FMS South Korea
F–16	88–0001–012	FMS Netherlands
F–16A	88–0016–018	FMS Denmark E016–E018
F–16A	88–0038–047	FMS Belgium FA113–FA123
F–16B	88–0048–49	FMS Belgium FB22–FB23
F–16A	89–0001–011	FMS Belgium FA124–FA133
F–16B	89–0012	FMS Belgium FB24
F–16A	89–0013–019	FMS Netherlands
F–16B	89–0020–021	FMS Netherlands
F–16A	89–0025–027	FMS Belgium FA134–FA136
F–16N	163268–281	US Navy

F–16 units

UNITED STATES

Direct Reporting Units

4485 TS	OT	F–16A	Black/white check	TAWC Eglin AFB
422 TES	57 FWW WA	F–16A/B	Yellow/black check	TFWC Nellis AFB
F–16 FWS	57 FWW WA Det II	F–16C/D	Yellow/black check	Luke AFB
64FWS	57 FWW	F–16A/B		Nellis AFB
to convert from F–5E/F to F–16A/B early 1989				
Thunderbirds		F–16A/B		Nellis AFB
318 FIS	25 AD 'TC'	F–16A/B		McChord
To convert from 18 × F–15A to 24 × F–16A late 1989				AFB

Tactical Air Command

9th Air Force

306 TFS	31 TFW ZF	F–16A/B	Yellow/white outline	Inactive
307 TFS*	31 TFW HS	F–16A/B	Red	Homestead AFB
308 TFS	31 TFW HS	F–16A/B	Green/white outline and name 'Wild Ducks'	Homestead AFB

309 TFS	31 TFW HS	F–16A/B	Blue/white outline	Homestead AFB

306th activated on F–16 in November 1985 but de-activated on 31 October 1986 and aircraft transferred to the 308TFS

61 TFTS	56 TTW MC	F–16C/D	Yellow/white outline	McDill AFB
62 TFTS	56 TTW MC	F–16A/B	Blue/white outline	McDill AFB
63 TFTS	56 TTW MC	F–16A/B	Red/white outline	McDill AFB
72 TFTS	56 TTW MC	F–16A/B	Black/white outline	McDill AFB

56TTW to begin receiving F–16C/D models late 1988

68 TFS	347 TFW MY	F–16A/B	Red	Moody AFB
69 TFS	347 TFW MY	F–16A/B	Silver	Moody AFB
70 TFS	347 TFW MY	F–16A/B	Blue/white checks	Moody AFB
17 TFS	363 TFW SW	F–16C/D	White/yellow edge	Shaw AFB
19 TFS	363 TFW SW	F–16C/D	Gold/black edge	Shaw AFB
33 TFS	363 TFW SW	F–16C/D	Blue	Shaw AFB

12th Air Force

4 TFS	388 TFW HL	F–16A/B	Yellow/red lightning	Hill AFB
16 TFS	388 TFW HL	F–16A/B	Blue/white check	In-active
34 TFS	388 TFW HL	F–16A/B	Red/'rams' in white	Hill AFB
421 TFS	388 TFW HL	F–16A/B	Black/red spider	Hill AFB
428 TFS	474 TFW NA	F–16A/B	Blue/white outline	Nellis AFB
429 TFS	474 TFW NA	F–16A/B	Black/yellow outline	Nellis AFB
430 TFS	474 TFW NA	F–16A/B	Red/white outline	Nellis AFB

474TFW to de-activate late 1988

832 Air Division

310 TFTS	58 TFW LF	F–16A/B	Green/gold outline	Luke AFB
311 TFTS	58 TFW LF	F–16A/B	Blue/white outline	Luke AFB
312 TFTS	58 TFW LF	F–16C/D	Black/red outline	Luke AFB
314 TFTS	58 TFW LF	F–16C/D	Yellow/black outline	Luke AFB
425 TFS	58 TFW LA	F–16A/B	to convert from F–5E/F to F–16A/B late 1989	

Pacific Air Force

5th Air Force

13 TFS	432 TFW MJ	F–16C/D	Black and white checks	Misawa AB
14 TFS	432 TFW MJ	F–16C/D	Black and yellow checks	Misawa AB

7th Air Force

35 TFS	8 TFW WP	F–16C/D	Blue	Kunsan AB
80 TFS	8 TFW WP	F–16C/D	Yellow	Kunsan AB
36 TFS*	51 TFW OS	F–16C/D	Red	Osan AB*

* 36th due to re-equip in late 1988

United States Air Force Europe

3rd Air Force

527 AS	81 TFW	F–16C/D	Red	Bentwaters

17th Air Force

10 TFS	50 TFW HR	F–16C/D	Blue	Hahn AB
313 TFS	50 TFW HR	F–16C/D	Orange	Hahn AB
496 TFS	50 TFW HR	F–16C/D	Yellow	Hahn AB
23 TFS	52 TFW SP	F–16C/D	Blue/white outline	Spangdahlen AB
81 TFS	52 TFW SP	F–16C/D	Yellow/black outline	Spangdahlen AB
480 TFS	52 TFW SP	F–16C/D	Red/white outline	Spangdahlen AB
512 TFS	86 TFW RS	F–16C/D	Green and black diagonal stripes	Ramstein AB

526 TFS	86 TFW RS '	F–16C/D	Black and red diagonal stripes	AB

16th Air Force

612 TFS	401 TFW TJ	F–16C/D	Blue and white checks	Torrejon AB
613 TFS	401 TFW TJ	F–16C/D	Yellow and black checks	Torrejon AB
614 TFS	401 TFW TJ	F–16C/D	Red and black checks	Torrejon AB

401 TFW will re-locate from Torrejon in 1989

Air National Guard

111 FIS	147 FIG	F–16A/B	Texas ANG	Ellington ANGB

to convert from 18 × F–4D to 18 × F–16A in 1990

114 TFTS	142 TFW	F–16A/B	Oregon ANG	Kingsley Field ANGB+
119 FIS	177 FIG	F–16A/B	New Jersey ANG	Atlantic City ANGB†
121 TFS	113 TFG 'DC'	F–16A/B	District of Columbia ANG	Andrews AFB

to convert from 24 × F–4D to 24 × F–16A in 1990

| 134 TFS | 158 TFG | F–16A/B | Vermont ANG | Burlington ANGB |
| 138 TFS | 174 TFG 'NY' | F–16A/B | New York ANG | Hancock Field Syracuse |

to convert from 24 × A–10A to 18 × F–16A mid–1989

157 TFS	169 TFG SC	F–16A/B	South Carolina Ang	McEntire ANGB
159 FIS	125 FIG	F–16A/B	Florida ANG	Jacksonville AP
160 TFS	187 TFG	F–16A/B	Alabama ANG	Montgomert AP+
161 TFTS	184 TFG	F–16A/B	Kansas ANG	McConnell AFB

171 FIS	119 FIG	F–16A/B	Michigan ANG	Selfridge ANGB

to convert from 18 × F–4D to 18 × F–16A in 1990

| 178 TFS | 119 FIG | F–16A/B | North Dakota ANG | Fargo (Hector Field) |

to convert from 18 × F–4D to 18 × F–16A in 1990

182 TFS	149 FG SA	F–16A/B	Texas ANG	Kelly AFB
184 TFS	188 TFG	F–16A/B	Arkansas ANG	Fort Smith AP+
186 FIS	120 FIG	F–16A/B	Montana ANG	Great Falls AP
194 FIS	144 FIG	F–16A/B	California ANG	Fresno AP

to convert from 18 × F–4D to 18 × F–16A in mid-1989

| 195 TFTS | 162 TFG | F–16A/B | Arizona ANG | Tucson ANGB |

+ 114 TFTS Oregon ANG due to re-equip early 1989
+ 160 TRS Alabama ANG due to re-equip spring 1988
+ 182 TFS Arkansa ANG due to re-equip spring 1988

Air Force Reserve

89 TFS		DO	F–16A/B		Wright-Patterson AFB+
93 TFS	915 TFG FM	F–16A/B			Homestead AFB+
302 TFS	944 TFG LR	F–16C/D	Yellow/red trident		Luke AFB linker AFB+
465 TFS	301 TFW TH	F–16A/B			
466 TFS	301 TFW HI	F–16A/B	Black and yellow diamonds		Hill AFB

+ 93 TFS and 465 TFS due to re-equip during FY88
+ 89 TFS due to re-equip during FY89

BELGIUM

1 'Smaldeel'	2 Wing	F–16A/B	–		Florennes+
2 'Smaldeel'	2 Wing	F–16A/B	–		Florennes+
23 'Smaldeel'	10 Wing	F–16A/B	Red/white diamonds		Kleine Brogel

31 'Smaldeel'	10 Wing	F–16A/B	Tiger's head	Kleine Brogel
349 'Smaldeel'	1 Wing	F–16A/B	Blue band	Beauvechain
350 'Smaldeel'	1 Wing	F–16A/B	Red band	Beauvechain

+2 Wing is due to re-equip 1988/89

DENMARK

Esk 723	F–16A/B		Aalborg
Esk 726	F–16A/B		Aalborg
Esk 727	F–16A/B		Skrydstrup
Esk 730	F–16A/B		Skrydstrup

NETHERLANDS

306 Sqn	F–16A/B	Eagle head on blue/black	Volkel
311 Sqn	F–16A/B	Black and white eagle on blue	Volkel
312 Sqn	F–16A/B	Crossed swords/red lightning	Volkel
313 Sqn	F–16A/B	Eagle on white runway/blue disc	Twenthe
315 Sqn	F–16A/B	Light grey lion on grey disc	Twenthe
322 Sqn	F–16A/B	Blue and grey parrot	Leeuwarden
323 Sqn	F–16A/B	Archer with red tunic, black disc	Leeuwarden
TCA	F–16A/B	Blue disc	Unit inactive

NORWAY

331 Skv	F–16A/B	Red/white/blue flash	Bodo
332 Skv	F–16A/B	Black/yellow flash	Rygge
334 Skv	F–16A/B	Red/white/blue flash	Bodo
338 Skv	F–16A/B	Black flash/yellow lightning	Rygge

F–16 Losses

??.??.??	72–1568	–	AFFTC
09.08.79	78–0078	HL	388 TFW
01.10.79	78–0006	HL	388 TFW
25.01.80	78–0071	HL	388 TFW
10.03.80	J216	–	–
26.03.80	78.0023	HL	388 TFW
23.07.80	78–0092	HL	388 TFW
28.07.80	FA08	–	349 Sqn/1 Wing
29.10.80	78–0110	MC	56 TTW
12.03.81	FA11	–	350 Sqn/1 Wing
27.03.81	78–0105	MC	56 TTW
06.04.81	78–0013	HL	388 TFW to GF–16A
10.04.81	79–0316	HL	388 TFW
02.06.81	280	–	*332 Skv*
03.06.81	J237	–	–
29.06.81	79–0313	HL	388 TFW
17.07.81	J217	–	323 Sqn
05.08.81	78–0046	HL	388 TFW
20.10.81	J233	–	–
22.10.81	FA29	–	349 Sqn/1 Wing
15.01.82	78–0048	HL	388 TFW
19.01.82	FA14	–	349 Sqn/1 Wing
19.01.82	FA35	–	350 Sqn/1 Wing
27.01.82	79–0318	HL	388 TFW
23.03.82	78–0112	–	3246 TW
12.04.82	78–0016	HL	388 TFW
04.05.82	79–0390	NA	474 TFW
11.05.82	78–0067	HL	388 TFW
20.05.82	79–0301	HL	388 TFW
20.05.82	79–0374	NA	474 TFW
09.06.82	79–0392	NA	474 TFW
16.06.82	79–0378	NA	474 TFW
06.07.82	80–0490	WP	8 TFW
08.11.82	79–0298	MC	56 TTW
01.12.82	80–0564	HR	50 TFW
15.12.82	81–0724	WP	8 TFW
27.12.82	79–0343	NA	474 TFW
12.01.83	80–0600	NA	474 TFW
19.01.83	79–0386	HL	388 TFW
20.01.83	80–0617	HR	50 TFW
31.01.83	283	–	*331 Skv*
10.02.83	80–0478	NA	474 TFW
21.03.83	J225	–	322 Sqn
05.04.83	E175	–	
26.04.83	J224	–	322 Sqn
26.04.83	J227	–	322 Sqn
10.05.83	81–0664	HR	50 TFW

Date	Serial	Code	Unit
10.05.83	FA13	–	349 Sqn/1 Wing
11.07.83	80-0627	MC	56 TTW
25.07.83	78-0113	MC	56 TTW
04.10.83	J252	–	322 Sqn
10.11.83	FA07	–	349 Sqn/1 Wing
10.11.83	FA41	–	349 Sqn/1 Wing
10.11.83	82-0925	HL	388 TFW
18.11.83	79-0390	NA	474 TFW
25.01.84	80-0595	WP	8 TFW
27.01.84	81-0730	HL	388 TFW
10.04.84	79-0313	SC	157 TFS
01.05.84	81-0745	HL	388 TFW
02.05.84	82-1045	HL	388 TFW
28.05.84	J634	–	311 Sqn
19.06.84	78-0072	MC	56 TTW
19.06.84	ET209	–	
19.06.84	ET211	–	
25.06.84	82-0971	TJ	401 TFW
19.09.84	FB16	–	10 Wing
25.09.84	80-0477	NA	474 TFW
12.11.84	82-0959	TJ	401 TFW
13.11.84	301	–	332 Skv
12.12.84	J271	–	TCA
??.??.85	82-1043	SW	363 TFW
07.02.85	79-0323	SC	157 TFS
08.02.85	81-0818	TJ	401 TFW
10.02.85	?	–	? /USAF
01.04.85	E179	–	Esk 730
01.04.85	E186	–	Esk 730
27.04.85	83-1117	SW	363 TFW
29.04.85	FA24	–	350 Sqn/1 Wing
16.05.85	79-0416	MC	56 TTW
03.06.85	J621	–	311 Sqn
03.06.85	J865	–	311 Sqn
12.06.85	303?	–	332 Skv
08.08.85	81-0750	HL	388 TFW
02.09.85	FA06	–	349 Sqn/1 Wing
22.10.85	80-0586	HR	50 TFW
01.11.85	79-0372	SW	363 TFW
15.11.85	82-0940	WA	57 FWW
15.11.85	82-1029	WA	57 FWW
11.12.85	78-0004	LF	58 TTW
12.02.86	78-0055	AD	3246 TW
27.02.86	83-1086	ZF	31 TTW
15.04.86	J629	–	306 Sqn
26.04.86.	?	–	? /USAF
13.06.86	J626	–	311 Sqn
30.06.86	FA79	–	23 Sqn/10 Wing
??.07.86	?	–	? /IDF
10.07.86	684	–	331 Skv
10.07.86	686	–	331 Skv
20.08.86	FA33	–	350 Sqn/1 Wing
11.09.86	?	WA	57 FWW
02.10.86	?	HI	466 TFS/afres (F-16A)
09.10.86	82-0998	TJ	401 TFW
09.10.86	84-1212	SW	363 TFW
10.10.86.	FA42	–	350 Sqn/1 Wing
12.11.86.	?	SW	363 TFW
17.11.86	J244	–	322 Sqn
30.12.86	?	–	? /PAF. An F-16B
22.03.87	83-1115	MJ	432 TFW
29.04.87	?	–	? /PAF. An F-16A
22.06.87	79-0385		
23.06.87	85-1424	RS	86 TFW
24.07.87	80-0597	WA	57 FWW
24.07.87	82-0912	WA	57 FWW
25.07.87	83-1149	SW	363 TFW
27.08.87	85-1517	RS	86 TFW
14.09.87	FA63	–	23 Sqn/10 Wing
15.09.87	?	–	338 Skv
17.09.87	84-1331	HR	50 TFW
19.09.87	FA52	–	350 Sqn/1 Wing
05.10.87	?	–	? /IDF
10.10.87	?	SW	363 TFW
19.10.87	85-1463	RS	86 TFW
02.11.87	84-1270	SW	363 TFW
07.12.87	E201	–	Esk 723
10.12.87	E185	–	Esk 730
17.12.87	83-1067	TJ	401 TFW
13.01.88	82-1015	TJ	401 TFW
11.02.88	J639	–	306 Sqn
20.02.88	86-0213	LR	302 TFS/afres
?.03.88	81-0766	HS	31 TTW
14.03.88	?	–	331 Skv
22.03.88	79-0397	MC	56 TTW
31.03.88	84-1389	HR	50 TFW
18.04.88	85-1462	RS	86 TFW
23.05.88	?	?	? /USAF
31.05.88	?	SA	182 TFS
04.06.88	J625	–	311 Sqn
07.06.88	81-0713	–	159 TFS
29.06.88	84-1395	HR	50 TFW
29.06.88	85-1401	HR	50 TFW
29.06.88	86-0247	SP	52 TFW
05.07.88	?	–	334 Skv

Back cover, above right
The F110 gives the F–16C a significant increase in thrust over the F100, which brings the heavier F–16C's performance more in line with the agile and lighter F–16A version. Here F–16C 85-1547/MJ of the 14th TFS, 432nd TFW touches down at Misawa AB in November 1987. *Peter R. Foster*

Back cover, below right
Unit markings on Danish aircraft are somewhat small and require close inspection to establish ownership, as illustrated by this *Esk 727* badge on the F–16's intake. *Herman J. Sixma*

Back cover, left
When the 1985 'Tiger Meet' was held at Kleine Brogel, No 31 Squadron specially painted FA62 in 'Tiger' stripes. However they were sensibly restricted from using anything other than a 'white wash' covering. This looked fine until the aircraft flew, then it all peeled off. *Herman J. Sixma*

Right
Fitted with wingtip smoke pods, this F–16C shows off its agility in a climbing turn whilst the vortices off the fuselage shows the 'g' being pulled. *Herman J. Sixma/IAAP*